ENGLISH

Homework

5

PHOTOCOPIABLE ACTIVITIES FOR USE AT HOME

Contents

How to use this book

- **Course:** this book of homework activity sheets is designed to be used with the *Password English* course. Each homework activity ties in with the core components of the course and is designed to be linked to classroom work. However, the homework activities could also be used independently, if required.

- **Home:** the activities in this book are specifically designed to be used at home. A minimal amount of resources and parental support is assumed, to enable the children to work as independently as possible. Obviously, those parents keen to assist their children and become involved in their homework should be encouraged to do so at every opportunity.

- **Time:** each activity should take up to about half an hour, although they are designed to be flexible and could take more or less time than this if required.

- **Strands:** three strands run throughout the activities in this book: home, interests/hobbies, and environment. Each activity focuses on one of these strands and uses it as the focal point of the work. The children could be encouraged to build up a portfolio of their homework throughout the year, grouped in the three strands.

- **Feedback:** space is provided to specify 'date set' and 'finish by'. Feedback from home should be encouraged, and space is provided in the wide left-hand margin of each sheet for the children or their parents to comment on the activity if necessary.

- **Flexibility:** above all, these homework activities are designed as flexible and adaptable additions to *Password English*, offering support, practice and extension of key English skills.

Spelling strategies ◆◆
Building words

Date set
_____

Finish by
_____

PCM
1

Name_____

Sometimes we can tell a word by its shape.

For example, this word could
be **book**, **head** or **look**!

1. Look at the puzzle below. All the shape words are to do with the outside of a house – the names of parts of the house and what they are made of.

2. Fill in the missing letters to make the words.

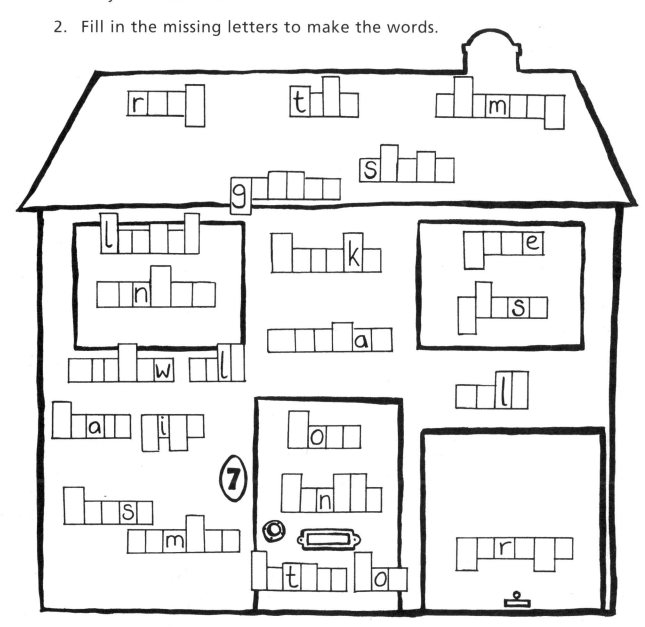

3. Now think of some words to describe the inside of a house. Use the back of this page to write your own shape words for these.

Plural nouns ◆◆

Stock-taking

Date set

_____

Finish by

_____

PCM
2

Name_____

Francesca's family own a small village shop. Every week, they do a check on all the stock. Today, she is checking a list her brother has written, but it is full of spelling mistakes!

1. Look at the spelling of each word in the list. Put a cross next to each incorrect word.

2. Write the correct spelling. The first one has been done for you.

10 packets biscuites   x

_____biscuits_____

15 fruit cakess

_____

20 loafs bread

_____

15 packets bread rolles

_____

20 packets plain crispss

_____

5 boxs cake mix

_____

10 packets jellys

_____

10 face clothes

_____

10 tins peachs

_____

10 tins peares

_____

5 punnets strawberrys

_____

5 bunchs bananas

_____

2 caulifloweres

_____

10 bags potatos

_____

10 jogurtes

_____

15 cartonns milk

_____

10 tub margarine

_____

2 legs of lamb (halfs)

_____

2 frozen lunchs

_____

5 bottls tomato sauce

_____

6 packets frozen French frys

_____

15 frozen pizzaes

_____

5 jares jam

_____

2 pocket knifes

_____

Prefixes and suffixes ◆◆
Travelling words

Name_____

Many transport and travelling words have **prefixes** that can help to explain the meaning of the word, e.g. **submarine** = *sub* (meaning 'under' or 'beneath') + *marine* (meaning 'found in the sea').

1. Work out the meaning of the following travelling words. Complete the table by writing in your definition of each word.

2. Use a dictionary to see if you are correct.

Prefix	Meaning	Word	Your definition
bi-	two	bicycle biplane	_____ _____
auto-	self, self-propelling	automobile autopilot	_____ _____
tri-	three	tricycle	_____
de-	remove	derail depart	_____ _____
multi-	many	multistorey	_____
circum-	around	circumnavigate	_____
mono-	one	monoplane monorail	_____ _____

3. How many other words can you find with these prefixes? Write the words and meanings on the back of this sheet.

ENGLISH

STAGE 5

Spelling rules ◆

In plentiful supply?

Date set
_____

Finish by
_____

PCM
4

Name_____

Will the world's resources always be in plentiful supply?
Many people think not. That is why we should always
try to use our resources wisely and recycle everything we can.

1. Complete the following sentences by choosing a
   word from the box and adding *full* to it.

   Remember:
   * *When we add -full to the end of a word, we have to
   drop one l, for example: arm + full = armful.*
   * *If a word ends in y, change the y to i before adding -ful, for example:
   bounty + full = bountiful.*

waste   wonder   plenty   harm   help   care   beauty   thank

   - We should be _____ to have so many
     _____ plants and animals in our world.

   - If we are _____ with our resources we will not run
     out of them.

   - The world is a _____ place. We should make sure it
     stays that way!

   - Paper will be in _____ supply if we recycle old
     paper.

   - It is _____ to re-use plastic carrier bags
     whenever possible.

   - Throwing away rubbish that can be recycled is
     _____ .

   - Many chemicals are _____ to our environment.

2. Now turn over and write three sentences about looking after our
   resources. Use adjectives made from these words:

   use + full   hope + full   dread + full

Sounds ◆◆

How do you say it?

Date set

_____

Finish by

_____

Name_____

One of Paula's hobbies is collecting words that have the same spelling but a different sound!

1. Help Paula match up each word below to a word on the right that has a similar sound. One has been done for you.

● **tough**	sounds like cuff	sloth
● d**ough**	sounds like go	nose
● b**ough**	sounds like cow	fear
● c**ough**	sounds like off	enough
● b**ear**	sounds like air	trough
● t**ear**	sounds like ear	whose
● **rose**	sounds like hose	though
● d**ose**	sounds like gross	froth
● l**ose**	sounds like ooze	plough
● m**oth**	sounds like Goth	pear
● b**oth**	sounds like growth	close

2. Sometimes, whole words are spelt the same but are pronounced differently and have a different meaning. These words are called **homographs**.

   Write a sentence about holidays for each of these words to show their different meanings.

   ● tear _____

   ● tear _____

   ● row _____

   ● row _____

ENGLISH
STAGE 5

Synonyms ◆◆

My home

Date set
_____

Finish by
_____

PCM
6

Name_____

Graham loves his house. He likes it so much that he has written a description of it for a glossy magazine called *Your House and Home*. The words Graham has used, however, could be improved.

1. Write a synonym for each word in **bold** in Graham's sentences below. Choose a word that is more interesting than Graham's. Use a thesaurus to help you if you wish.

   Remember: a synonym is a word that is similar in meaning to another word, for example: friend – chum, pal, buddy, mate, companion.

   - My house is **big** _____.

   - It has a **nice** _____ garden and a **good** _____ view.

   - The rooms are very **large** _____.

   - The hallway is **big** _____ and **wide** _____ with lots of space to hang your coats.

   - The living room is **good** _____ because it has a **nice** _____ open fire-place.

   - The kitchen is **great** _____. It has a **big** _____ table so we can all eat together.

   - We have two **large** _____ bathrooms which are **nicely** _____ decorated.

2. How would you describe your home? Write five sentences about it on the back of this sheet.

   Try to use words that make it sound exciting and interesting!

ENGLISH
STAGE 5

Common expressions ◆◆
Mr Blackaby's sayings

Date set
_____

Finish by
_____

PCM
7

Name_____

Old Mr Blackaby is always coming up with lots of strange expressions and old sayings. Some of these are shown below.

1. Work out what the following sayings mean.
   The first one has been done for you.

It's raining cats and dogs.

It's raining very hard.
_____

Hold your horses!

_____
_____
_____

You are driving me up the wall!

_____
_____
_____

I've decided to turn over a new leaf.

_____
_____
_____

Don't beat about the bush!

_____
_____
_____

I'm all ears.

_____
_____
_____

2. Now turn over and write some interesting sayings of your own for each of these meanings:

   ● to move very fast   ● to have lots of experience
   ● to be very fit   ● to be very old

Computer words

Date set

_____

Finish by

_____

PCM
8

Name_____

Ahmed loves computers! Try this computer word challenge he has written.

Look at the sentences, then write the number of the correct definition in the boxes next to the words.

Remember: _many computer words are actually_ **acronyms** _(words which are made up from the letters of other words, for example: CAD = Computer-Aided Design)._

byte	6	_BASIC_	☐	_modem_	☐	_network_	☐
software	☐	_RAM_	☐	_hardware_	☐	_VDU_	☐

1. Beginner's All-purpose Symbolic Instruction Code – a computer language.

2. A device used to connect a computer to a telephone.

3. The data and programs that a computer uses.

4. Two or more computers linked up so that they work together.

5. Visual Display Unit – a screen similar to a television screen.

6. A measure of a computer's memory, equal to 8 bits.

7. All the working parts of a computer including the disk drive, keyboard and printer.

8. Random Access Memory – stores programs and data while work is being done on the computer.

Now turn over and write your own definitions of these words:
keyboard, database, CD-ROM.

Special words ◆◆
Making sounds

Date set
_____

Finish by
_____

Name_____

What sounds do you hear when you visit the seaside?
Sometimes the words we use to describe these sounds actually
sound like the noise itself. Words that sound like the noise things
make are called **onomatopoeia**.

1. Look at the following examples.

splashing	gurgling	sigh	squelch	crashing	roaring

2. Read the poem below out loud to hear the sounds the words make:

The gurgling, hissing, tumbling waves
Came crashing, pounding to the shore.
There they gently whispered and sighed,
Then rushed back out to return once more.

3. Write a list of onomatopoeic words to describe the following:

walking through deep mud in wellingtons	running through dried leaves in a wood	watching a firework display

4. Now use the lists of words to write your own short poem about
   mud, woodland sounds or fireworks. Write it on the back of this
   sheet. Include as many onomatopoeic words as you can!

Special words ◆◆

From the French

Name_____

Tom's family often go on holiday to France.
He has discovered that lots of French words
are also used in the English language.
Look at these examples.

1. café	2. silhouette
3. camouflage	4. brochure
5. chalet	6. garage

Use these French words in
sentences to show their meaning.
Use a dictionary to help you.

1. _____

_____

2. _____

_____

3. _____

_____

4. _____

_____

5. _____

_____

6. _____

_____

Now find two more French words that are used in the English
language. Turn over and use them in sentences.

ENGLISH

STAGE 5

Antonyms ◆◆

Neighbourhood report

Name_____

Date set
_____

Finish by
_____

PCM
11

Martina has been asked to write a report about her neighbourhood. Unfortunately, she is not very happy about what she will have to write because her local environment has not been well looked after.

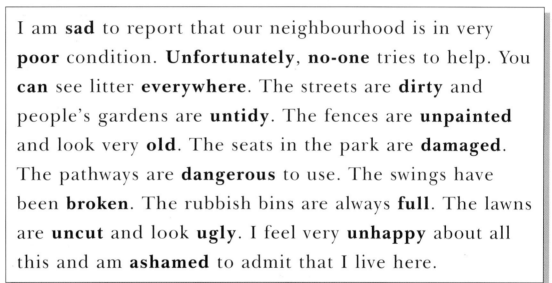

1. Read Martina's report to find out why she is unhappy.

I am **sad** to report that our neighbourhood is in very **poor** condition. **Unfortunately**, **no-one** tries to help. You **can** see litter **everywhere**. The streets are **dirty** and people's gardens are **untidy**. The fences are **unpainted** and look very **old**. The seats in the park are **damaged**. The pathways are **dangerous** to use. The swings have been **broken**. The rubbish bins are always **full**. The lawns are **uncut** and look **ugly**. I feel very **unhappy** about all this and am **ashamed** to admit that I live here.

2. Now make Martina happy by rewriting her report! Copy out her report and write an *antonym* (opposite) for every word in bold.

_____

_____

_____

_____

_____

_____

3. How could your neighbourhood be improved?
    Write some ideas on the back of this sheet.

Standard English ◆◆
Moving day

Date set
_____

Finish by
_____

PCM
12

Name_____

Last week, John's family moved house.
When they came to unpack, everyone had a
lot of trouble deciding who owned what!

Find out how much trouble everyone had
by completing the sentences below. Select
the correct possessive pronoun from the
box so that each sentence makes sense.

*Remember: possessive pronouns show
belonging, for example: It is **his** book.*

my	mine	your	yours	his	her
hers	its	our	ours	their	theirs

1. "That's not _____ jumper, it's _____," declared Michael.

2. "Take these up to Sarah's room. I'm sure they are _____,"
    said Dad.

3. "Yuck, that towel has _____ own particular smell! It must be the
    dog's!" said John.

4. "That's _____ and this is _____," Peter told John.

5. "_____ football boots are missing," wailed John and Peter.

6. "Tell Pauline I found _____ paint set," said Mum.

7. "Ask the boys to put away _____ roller blades!" yelled Dad.

8. "Pauline, ask John to find _____ camera. I want a photo of this
    chaos!" laughed Mum.

Use the back of this sheet to write three more sentences using
possessive pronouns.

Verbs ◆

Aunt Flo's mix-ups

PCM
13

Name_____

Aunt Flo is always getting her words confused! Sometimes, she mixes up the past and future! Look at this example:

I filled the vase with water. *(past tense)*

I will fill the vase with water. *(future tense)*

1. Rewrite Aunt Flo's sentences by changing the verbs in brackets into the **past** tense.

   - All the shops in town (are) _____ busy.

   - I (shall practise) _____ my recorder for the concert.

   - No-one (knows) _____ why Aunt Gladys (is) _____ out today.

2. Rewrite these sentences by changing the verbs in brackets into the **present** tense.

   - Uncle Ivan (left) _____ for his holiday today.

   - My brother (will be learning) _____ how to fly.

   - That story (was) _____ often repeated.

3. Now rewrite Aunt Flo's sentences by changing the verbs in brackets into the **future** tense:

   - The birthday cake (is) _____ delicious.

   - I (am learning) _____ German at the new college.

   - Susan (left) _____ early in the morning.

Turn over and write two sentences each in the past, present and future tenses, all about your family.

ENGLISH
STAGE 5

Word order ◆◆

Star gazing

Date set

_____

Finish by

_____

PCM
14

Name_____

Michelle really enjoys learning about astronomy. She has been asked to write about her interest for a class book, but her sentences are too long and are full of unnecessary words.

1. Help Michelle to edit her report by crossing out all the words that are not essential.

    Our planet, planet Earth, is one of the planets in our solar system. The solar system is a system made up of nine planets and the Sun. The hot Sun is enormously huge like a gigantic hot ball of hot fire. The order of the nine planets from the Sun is: planet Mercury, the closest planet to the Sun, planet Venus, the second planet from the Sun, planet Earth, the third planet from the Sun, planet Mars, the fourth planet from the Sun, planet Jupiter, the fifth planet from the Sun, planet Saturn, the sixth planet from the Sun, planet Uranus, the seventh planet from the Sun, planet Neptune, the eighth planet from the Sun and planet Pluto, the ninth planet from the Sun. All the planets travel round and round the Sun in an orbit.

2. Now rewrite the report so that it includes only the essential words. You can change or re-order some words to improve the sentences, but don't change the meaning! Continue on the back of the sheet.

    _____

    _____

    _____

    _____

Grammar strategies ◆◆

Birthday surprise

Date set

_____

Finish by

_____

PCM
15

Name_____

1. Naomi is making her younger brother, Paul, a little book as a surprise for his birthday. Paul is very fond of animals, so Naomi has decided to make him a book about the Red Squirrel using the information below.

> * *Description* – Red Squirrels have a reddish-brown coat with white underparts. They have large, pointed tufted ears. Hind legs are much larger than forelimbs. Feet well adapted for climbing.
> * *Habitat* – particularly likes coniferous woodlands but also lives in mixed woods throughout most of Europe.
> * *Food* – mainly vegetarian. Eats seeds, including acorns and chestnuts, as well as fungi, insects and bird's eggs.
> * *Habits* – nests in dome-shaped drays made of twigs, bark, moss and leaves.

2. Rewrite the information in simpler words and sentences so that Paul will understand it.

_____

_____

_____

_____

3. Turn over and draw a picture to go with the information for Paul.

ENGLISH

STAGE 5

Direct and reported speech ◆◆

News report

Date set

_____

Finish by

_____

PCM
16

Name_____

Cassandra wants to be a news reporter on television, so she likes to practise recording conversations to write up as news reports later. Help her to write up a recorded conversation.

1. Read through this conversation.

> "I want to welcome everyone to this meeting," said Mr Brown. "Mrs Slocombe, would you like to speak first?"
>
> "Thank you. I am very concerned about this new factory being built near our homes. It will cause pollution and will look ugly," replied Mrs Slocombe.
>
> "I agree – I know that we need work," said Mr Smith, "but why does the factory have to be built so close?"
>
> "It's the best site available,",Mr Knight replied. "Our survey shows your town is the very best place for such a new and exciting factory."
>
> "Would you like to live next door to it?" asked Mrs Slocombe angrily.
>
> "Please stay calm, everyone, " said Mr Brown. "We'll take a vote to decide what to do."

2. Now rewrite the conversation in reported speech. Continue on the back of this sheet. The first sentence has been written for you.

<u>Mr Brown said that he wanted to welcome everyone to the meeting.</u>

_____

_____

_____

_____

_____

Sentence structure ◆◆
Weird headlines!

Name_____

Newspaper headlines often use shortened sentences. Sometimes, this makes the meaning unclear.

Look at this example:

DOG HIT BY CAR RUNNING ACROSS ROAD

Does this mean that a dog was hit by a car which ran across the road? Or does it mean that a dog ran across the road and was hit by a car?

1. Write what you think these headlines really mean.

POLICE SHOOT MAN WITH KNIFE

_____

MAN ESCAPES ON A HORSE EATING A BURGER

_____

MAN CHASES SHEEP IN CAR

_____

MILLIONAIRE MARRIES GIRL IN SHOP

_____

DOG BITES MAN WITH BIG TEETH

_____

2. Use the back of this page to write some weird headlines of your own! Draw pictures to go with each one!

PASSWORD
ENGLISH
STAGE 5

Sentence structure ◆◆

Next door

Date set
_____

Finish by
_____

PCM
18

Name_____

Make one sentence from these pairs of sentences
using the words **who**, **whose**, **which** or **that**.
The first one has been done for you.

1. Our neighbour returned yesterday. He had been on holiday.

   Our neighbour, who had been on holiday, returned yesterday.

2. Our neighbour looked very tired. His bag was very heavy.

   _____

3. He opened the front door. It creaked very loudly.

   _____

4. The man went into the house. It is very large and spooky.

   _____

5. Then we heard strange noises. The noises were very loud.

   _____

6. Our dog barked very loudly and ran to the house. His chain
   had broken.

   _____

7. Our dog scratched at the door. Our dog was very excited.

   _____

8. The neighbour shouted at our dog. Our dog ran away
   looking very scared.

   _____

Now turn over and write two more
sentences to complete the story!

Sentence structure ◆◆

Tall tales

Name _____

Have you ever stretched the truth in order to show off to someone? Jeremy is always telling tall tales to impress his friends. Look at some of the things he has told them below.

Make sense of Jeremy's sentences by putting in the commas.

Remember: commas are used in lists and when we want to add more detail about something.
For example: Fred bought apples, pears, bananas and apricots.
Fred, the boy next door, bought lots of fruit.

1. I own five dogs six cats twenty-four budgies and eighteen frogs!

2. My uncle who once managed Manchester United is the greatest footballer alive today!

3. Steven my brother is taller than a telephone box braver than a lion and smarter than a fox!

4. Our house hidden by huge trees has more flowers than a botanical garden!

5. Our car can go faster than a BMW a Mercedes or a Formula One racing car!

6. Although I am only ten I can play a guitar a violin and a piano.

7. My dog Rover can run twenty miles without stopping climb trees and sing along to music!

8. I never tell lies well hardly ever I just stretch the truth a little!

Now turn over and write two sentences with tall tales of your own!

Prepositions ◆◆

Animal sentences

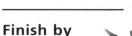
Name_____

A preposition is a word that shows the relationship between a noun or pronoun and some other word in a sentence. Here are some examples of prepositions.

along	outside	near
in	on	behind
next to	inside	beneath
with	across	through
against	under	before
below	by	beyond

Change the prepositions in these sentences so that the sentences still make sense.

1. The horse galloped <u>through</u> the open field and <u>down</u> the lane.

    The horse galloped _____ the open field and _____ the lane.

2. The cat sat <u>on</u> the wall <u>near</u> the tree <u>beside</u> me.

    The cat sat _____ the wall _____ the tree _____ me.

3. <u>Beside</u> the river, <u>underneath</u> a huge tree

    we found a spider <u>inside</u> a log.

    _____ the river, _____ a huge tree

    we found a spider _____ a log.

4. <u>Beyond</u> our house we could see a dove

    sitting <u>near</u> the posts of a fence.

    _____ our house we could see a dove

    sitting _____ the posts of a fence.

Certain prepositions always follow certain words, such as:

similar to   *responsible for*   *different from*

Turn over and write three sentences about animals using these words.

ENGLISH
STAGE 5

Punctuation revision ◆◆
My home town

Date set
_____

Finish by
_____

PCM
21

Name_____

Jane enjoys living in her home town. She has written a description of it below. Unfortunately, all of the punctuation is missing!

1. Put in all the capital letters, full stops, commas, apostrophes and colons to complete the description.

    Remember: a colon (:) can be used to introduce a list, for example:
    The boy needs three things: a book, a pencil and a ruler.

i live in a small town called amesborough it is a pretty town with lots of trees flowers and parks there is a town hall a post office a shopping centre two pubs a sports centre and a cinema so theres always something to do here i like to ride my bike to the sports centre and go swimming the town hall which is very old usually has an art or craft exhibition each week my mum who is an artist sometimes sells her paintings there my dad works at the post office so he knows nearly everyone in the town he thinks our town has three good points beautiful buildings friendly people and a kind post-master i enjoy living here because it feels safe and friendly amesborough has a flower festival and fair every year to raise money for the large town church last year my dad won first prize for the best roses i entered two competitions best painting and best costume unfortunately i did not win anything

2. What is your village, town or city like to live in?
    Use the back of this sheet to write a description of
    where you live. Remember to put in all the punctuation!

Dialogue ◆◆
Netball match

Name_____

1. Natalie has written about the school netball match for her friend Rosie, who missed the game. Natalie is unsure of where to put the speech marks and commas. Help by putting them in for her.

Today, Blue team are playing St. John's School. The whistle is blown and the game begins. The Blue team take the ball. Jane passes it to Tom who then looks around for his team mate, Sheree.

Here Tom shouts Sheree I'm over here!

Get in front Sheree, get in front shouts Tom.

Well done Sheree says Tom. Now pass it to Louise.

Louise grabs the ball in time, swivels around on one foot and scores a goal.

Hooray shouts the Blue team.

Come on Blues says Ahmed we can do it again.

This time, however, the St. John's team are doing really well and soon have control of the ball.

Pass it to me quick shouts the Centre. I'm right here.

Good now pass it to Sara shouts the Centre.

Yes we did it we've scored a goal shouts the St. John's team.

2. Turn over and write the end of the story. Remember to use all the correct punctuation marks!

PASSWORD ENGLISH STAGE 5

Apostrophes ♦♦

The circus

Date set

_____

Finish by

_____

PCM
23

Name _____

Read this text about Michael's trip to the circus. Add in all the apostrophes in the correct places.

Michaels excitement was very clear when he found out they were going on a days outing to the circus. They took mums car and after an hours drive, they arrived at Jones Circus, the newest circus to hit the country.

Dad took Michaels hand as they entered the huge crowded circus tent.

"Dont let go until we find a seat," said Michaels dad as they collected their tickets.

"I wont, dont worry dad. I dont want to get lost yet!" replied Michael.

They were soon seated and a trumpets blast announced the beginning of the opening parade. Ten clowns tumbled into the ring followed by four acrobats turning somersaults. The spectators laughter was deafening. Michael laughed until he thought his sides would split.

Then the drums rolled and some trapeze artists had their turn. They swung from each others feet and did somersaults in the air. At one time, Michael thought one was going to fall. A gasp escaped from the crowds lips, but the performer didnt hurt himself; he landed safely in his partners arms.

A strong man lifted people high into the air and a man on stilts jumped over the heads of a long line of people. The circus band perfomed several tunes and then the entertainment was over. Everyone had enjoyed themselves and Michael was very pleased with his days outing.

PASSWORD
ENGLISH
STAGE 5

Authors ◆◆
Author survey

Date set

_____

Finish by

_____

PCM
24

Name_____

1. Carry out this survey with members of your family.

   ● How many popular classic authors have they read or heard of?

   ● Talk to grandparents or older people as part of your survey if possible.

   ● Write the total 'yes' responses in each box. If someone has heard of the book but not read it, it still counts!

   Treasure Island by Robert Louis Stevenson ☐   *Famous Five* by Enid Blyton ☐

   Just William by Richmal Crompton ☐   *Fairy Tales* by Hans Christian Anderson ☐

   Alice's Adventures in Wonderland by Lewis Carroll ☐   *The Secret Garden* by Frances Hodgson Burnett ☐

   The Railway Children by E. Nesbit ☐   *Black Beauty* by Anna Sewell ☐

   The Adventures of Tom Sawyer by Mark Twain ☐   *The Lion, The Witch and the Wardrobe* by C. S. Lewis ☐

2. Use the back of this page to answer these questions:

   ● Which titles have been read or heard of by all or most of your family?

   ● Which book is your favourite? Why?

   ● Interview an older family member or friend. What is his or her favourite children's book? Does he or she think it would appeal to children today? Why?

PASSWORD
ENGLISH
STAGE 5

Playscripts ◆◆

Drama competition

Date set
_____

Finish by
_____

PCM
25

Name_____

The local theatre is holding a play-writing competition for children. The winning play will be performed on the opening night to a live audience!

1. You have been asked to enter the competition. Choose your topic from those listed below:

Alien Invasion!	*The Magic Football*
The Haunted House	*The Mad Dog*
The Surprise	*Nightmare Holiday*

2. You need four main characters in your play. Write their names here:

a) _____   c) _____

b) _____   d) _____

3. Write notes on the setting of your play here.

_____

_____

_____

_____

4. Write notes on the plot of your play here.

_____

_____

_____

5. Now turn over and write the beginning of your play.

Characters ◆◆

Characters from *Matilda*

Date set

_____

Finish by

_____

PCM
26

Name_____

Miss Honey and Miss Trunchbull are the teachers from Roald Dahl's book, Matilda.

1. Read these extracts about them:

> **Miss Honey**
>
> Miss Jennifer Honey was a mild and quiet person who never raised her voice and was seldom seen to smile, but there is no doubt she possessed that rare gift for being adored by every small child under her care. She seemed to understand totally the bewilderment and fear that so often overwhelms young children who for the first time in their lives are herded into a classroom and told to obey orders.

> **Miss Trunchbull**
>
> Miss Trunchbull, the headmistress, was something else altogether. She was a gigantic holy terror, a fierce monster who frightened the life out of the pupils and teachers alike. When she came up close you could almost feel the dangerous heat radiating from her as from a red-hot rod of metal.

Answer these questions on the back of this sheet.

2. What kind of person do you think Miss Honey is in this story? Explain your answer by referring to the extracts.

3. List the words and phrases that tell you that Miss Honey is a nice person and Miss Trunchbull is not.

4. Are the names Miss Honey and Miss Trunchbull well-suited to their characters? Explain why.

5. What sentence tells us that Mrs Honey is not happy with life? Why do you think this is?

ENGLISH
STAGE 5

Structure ◆◆

The family

Date set
_____

Finish by
_____

**PCM
27**

Name_____

1. Read the beginnings of these stories. They are all about families.

A	B
Once upon a time, long ago, on the edge of a great forest, there lived two brothers who were swineherds. The elder brother was very unkind to the younger brother called Jack; he made him do all the work and gave him hardly enough to eat. Philippa Pearce *The Squirrel-Wife*	All the way up the stairs, the children fought not to carry the envelope. Towards the top, Lydia took advantage of her height to force it down Christopher's jumper. Christopher pulled it out and tried to thrust it into Natalie's hand. "Here, Natty," he said. "Give this to Dad." Anne Fine *Madam Doubtfire*

2. Which story beginning do you prefer? Why?

    _____

3. What kind of story do you think story **A** will be? How might it end?

    _____

4. Do you like stories to begin right in the middle of the action, as in story **B**, or do you prefer to be introduced to the characters first, as in story **A**? Give your reasons why.

    _____

    _____

5. Turn over and write the beginning of a story about your own family.

PASSWORD
ENGLISH
STAGE 5

Reading strategies ◆◆
My thoughts on reading

Date set
_____

Finish by
_____

PCM
28

Name_____

Answer these questions about reading.

1. What types of books do you prefer to read? Why?

_____

_____

_____

2. Do you think reading is important? Why?

_____

_____

_____

3. What kinds of books do you dislike reading? Why?

_____

_____

_____

4. What kinds of things do you think you can learn from reading stories?

_____

_____

5. Do you enjoy reading books with pictures or do you prefer to imagine the places and characters in your head?

_____

6. If you could recommend one book to a friend, what would it be? Why?

_____

_____

Traditional stories ◆◆
Solving problems

Name_____

Date set
_____

Finish by
_____

PCM
29

Sometimes, listening to stories can help us to solve our problems. Fables are short stories that aim to help people in their daily lives. *Aesop's Fables* are very well known.

1. Look at the following fable called *The Boy who Cried Wolf*.

A shepherd boy, who wanted some amusement during the long days he spent out on the hillside guarding his sheep, decided to play a joke on his neighbours. He shouted "Wolf, wolf!" at the top of his voice, so that he was heard in the village below. The villagers left their work and ran up the hill to help him, thinking that wolves were attacking his flock. The boy laughed and thought this was a good trick.

The next day, the boy decided to see if he could get the villagers up the hill again. He called "Wolf, wolf!", and again, several good-hearted people came out to see if he was in trouble. On the third day, the wolves came. The boy cried "Wolf, wolf!" but nobody came to help him, and his sheep were destroyed.

The moral of this fable is that if you make a lot of fuss about nothing all the time, no-one will believe you when you have real problems.

Aesop's Fables, retold by Jacqueline Morley

2. Write a modern-day version of the fable on the back of this sheet.

● You can change the characters and setting but keep the message the same.

● Keep your fable short, and remember that fables always have animals in them.

STAGE 5

Point of view ♦♦
The factory

Date set

Finish by

PCM
30

Name_____

Would you like to live next door to a big factory?
What advantages and disadvantages might there be?

1. Read this account by a factory owner to find
   out his point of view.

   This factory has provided hundreds of local
   people with employment. The factory does
   cause pollution, I agree, but surely it's better
   to have some pollution than have lots of people
   out of work! The factory is noisy, but this is a town after all,
   you've got to expect noise if you live here. If people don't want
   any noise they should live in the country.

   I'm proud of the things we make here. We use local
   products and we sell our goods all over the world. This helps our
   whole country. Some people complain that the smoke from the
   factory causes them to get asthma but I think cars cause more
   problems than we do. This factory has been here a long time and
   I think it should stay here forever!

2. Now imagine that you are the chairman of the local resident's
   committee. The people have asked you to speak to the factory
   owner about the problems the factory causes.

   - Write what you might say and how you think things could
     be improved.

   - Continue on the back of the sheet.

   _____

   _____

   _____

   _____

Genres ◆◆

The haunted house

Date set

_____

Finish by

_____

PCM
31

Name_____

You have been asked to write a spooky story about a haunted house!

1. Look at these ideas for writing your story:

Ideas for plot/setting	Things to write about
Very large old house with lots of bedrooms, a cellar and attic.	Describe the house and gardens.
New people move in.	Describe the family.
Strange things happen.	Write about the strange happenings – what went on? How did the family feel/behave?
The youngest child in the family sees a ghost, but no-one else does.	Who was the ghost? Why was he/she haunting the house?
The child and the ghost become friends.	Why was it that only one child could see the ghost?
The child and the ghost play a trick on the rest of the family.	What trick did they play on the family?
The family decide to stay in the house and live with the ghost.	

2. Write the beginning of your story here. Continue on the back of the page. Try to make your story sound scary!

_____

_____

_____

_____

_____

ENGLISH
STAGE 5

Cultures and traditions ◆◆
Grandad's favourite poem

Date set
_____
Finish by
_____

PCM
32

Name_____

Shireen's Grandad loves poems. He can remember some of them off by heart!

1. Read this favourite poem of Grandad's.

Crabbed Age and Youth

Crabbed Age and Youth
Cannot live together:
Youth is full of pleasance,
Age is full of care;
Youth like summer morn,
Age like winter weather;
Youth like summer brave,
Age like winter bare;
Youth is full of sport,
Age's breath is short;
Youth is nimble, Age is lame;
Youth is hot and bold,
Age is weak and cold,
Youth is wild, and Age is tame.

William Shakespeare

---

2. Write those words in the poem which you think are no longer commonly used.

_____

_____

_____

_____

3. What do you think each of these words means? Write your ideas.

_____

_____

_____

_____

4. Look at the lines 'Youth is full of sport' and 'Youth is hot and bold'. What do you think these lines mean? Explain your ideas below.

_____

_____

_____

_____

Forms of poetry ◆◆

Body parts

Date set
_____

Finish by
_____

PCM
33

Name_____

Words that can have two different meanings are called **homonyms**. Read the lines from this poem that use homonyms.

Foolish questions

Where can a man buy a cap for his knee?

Or a key for a lock of his hair?

What jewels are found in the crown of his head

And who walks on the bridge of his nose?

Can the crook of his elbow be sent to jail –

If it can, well, then, what did it do?

Can he sit in the shade of the palm of his hand,

And beat time with the drum in his ear?

American folk rhyme (adapted)

1. Write a sentence to show the different meanings of these words. The first one has been done for you.

   ● neck   The boy hurt his neck when he fell.

            The neck of the wine bottle was covered in candle wax.

   ● chest   _____

            _____

   ● bottom _____

            _____

   ● feet   _____

            _____

2. Turn over and write the names of other body parts that can have different meanings.

3. Now use the words and sentences to provide ideas for a short poem about body parts.

Forms of poetry ◆◆
Describing our world

Name_____

1. Read the poem below which uses many similes.

The Fly

How large unto the tiny fly
Must little things appear!
– A rosebud like a feather
    bed,
Its prickle like a spear,
A dewdrop like a looking-
    glass
A hair like golden wire;
The smallest grain of
    mustard-seed
As fierce as coals of fire;
A loaf of bread, a lofty hill;
A wasp, a cruel leopard;
And specks of salt as bright
    to see
As lambkins to a shepherd.

Walter de la Mare

Remember: a simile says something is **like** something else, and often uses the words 'like' or 'as'.
A metaphor says something **is** something else. Look at these two examples:
simile – 'The calm sea shone **like** a mirror'
metaphor – 'The raging sea **is** a hungry beast.'

2. Choose one simile from the poem and rewrite it as a metaphor. For example: *'Its prickle like a spear'* could become *'It's prickle is a sword'*.

_____

_____

_____

_____

3. Write some similes and metaphors of your own. Think carefully about each item to find an appropriate description.

- The flower is like _____

- A new born lamb is _____

- The mountain is _____

- The galloping horse is like _____

- The fish swim as fast as _____

Classic poetry ◆◆
Colonel Fazackerley

Name_____

A narrative poem tells us a story. Below are the first and last verses of a narrative poem about a character called Colonel Fazackerley. The Colonel moves into his castle and discovers a ghost. Instead of being afraid, the Colonel finds the ghost amusing and tries to make friends with it. The ghost becomes so frustrated it can't scare the Colonel that it leaves!

1. Read these verses.

Colonel Fazackerley

Colonel Fazackerley
   Butterworth-Toast
Bought an old castle
   complete with a ghost,
But someone or other
   forgot to declare
To Colonel Fazack that
   the spectre was there.

_____

"Oh dear, what a pity!"
   said Colonel Fazack.
"I don't know his name,
   so I can't call him back."
And then with a smile
   that was hard to define,
Colonel Fazackerley went
   in to dine.

Charles Causley

---

2. Now write two verses of your own for the middle of the poem, telling the story of how Colonel Fazackerley upsets the ghost.

- Remember that the poem has rhyming couplets, so the last words rhyme in each pair of lines – e.g. *toast/ghost*.

- Use these couplets to help you if you wish, or write your own verses on the back of this page.

The spectre appeared on the very first day

Well *hello*, said the Colonel, I do hope you'll stay!

_____

_____

The shivering spectre still wailed and cried

But the Colonel simply laughed, smiled and sighed

_____

_____

Classic poetry ◆◆

The waterfall

Date set

_____

Finish by

_____

PCM
36

Name_____

Writers and poets often describe things in unusual ways. This writer has used language imaginatively to describe a waterfall.

1. Look carefully at the words the writer uses.

The thunderous noise of the waterfall could be heard well before we stepped out in front of it. Sparkling droplets of spray covered us like tiny diamonds twinkling in the sunlight. The force of the water cascading onto the rocks below echoed through our bodies as we stood watching. Water hitting the rocks bounced high into the air like exploding firecrackers only to drift away in a steamy mist. Whirlpools of water twisted and twirled angrily before rushing away down into the stream beyond.

2. Write two sentences from the text that use similes.

    _____

    _____

3. Which sentence do you like best in the text? Copy it out here and say why you like the words and phrases used.

    _____

    _____

4. Can water really move 'angrily'? Why do you think the author has used this word to describe the water?

    _____

5. Use some ideas from this text to write a short poem about a waterfall on the back of this sheet.

Performance poetry ◆◆
Football poems

Date set

_____

Finish by

_____

PCM
37

PASSWORD
ENGLISH
STAGE 5

Name_____

1. Read these poems. They are all about football.

Picking teams
When we pick teams in the
  playground,
Whatever the game might be,
There's always somebody left until last
And usually it's me.

I stand there looking hopeful
And tapping myself on the chest,
But the captains pick the others first,
Starting, of course, with the best.

Maybe if teams were sometimes
  picked
Starting with the worst,
Once in his life a boy like me
Could end up being first!

              Allan Ahlberg

Unfair
When we went over the park
Sunday mornings
To play football
we picked up sides.

Lizzie was our striker
because she had the best
  shot.
When the teachers
chose the school team
Marshy was our striker.

Lizzie wasn't allowed to play,
they said.
So she watched us lose,
  instead...

              Michael Rosen

2. Which poem do you like best? Give your reasons why.

_____

_____

3. Why do you think Michael Rosen's poem is called 'Unfair'?

_____

_____

4. Which poem would you choose to put in an anthology of football
poems? Turn over and give your reasons why.

Recounted texts ◆◆

The robber

Date set
_____

Finish by
_____

Name_____

1. Your local shop has been robbed! Look at the picture of the robber below.

2. Write a short description of the robber by looking carefully at the drawing. Include these things in your description:
   - approximate age
   - hair colour/style
   - special facial features
   - clothing worn
   - type of shoes
   - what he was carrying.

   _____

   _____

   _____

   _____

   _____

   _____

   _____

   _____

3. Now imagine you were an eye-witness to the robbery. Write a detailed account of what happened, using the back of this sheet. Include this information:

   - the name and location of the shop
   - time of robbery
   - the people in the shop

   - what the robber did
   - what the robber stole
   - how the robber escaped.

Instructions ◆◆

Making a water garden

Date set
_____

Finish by
_____

PCM
39

Name_____

Jonathan enjoys gardening. His grandad does, too, and he recently wrote to Jonathan telling him how to make his own miniature water garden.

1. Read his grandfather's letter.

> 29 Smith Street
> Greenton GR9 1BD
>
> 12 May
>
> Dear Jonathan,
> Here's all you need to know to make the water garden I told you about. Go to the garden centre and buy some water weeds, a water-lily in a pot, some water snails and some small goldfish. Remember that old laundry tub your mother used to use? Well, clean that out or use a large plastic baby's bath. Decide where you want the water garden. It's best in a sunny but sheltered spot. Put a layer of soil in the bottom of the tub about 10 cm deep.
>
> Then fill the tub with water and let it stand for a while so that the soil sinks back to the bottom. Plant the water weeds into the soil and use a small stone to anchor them. Next, put in the water-lily. It can stay in its pot as it will soon grow up to the surface. Leave the tub to stand for a few days. Then put in the water snails and fish. You will now have your own little pond! I hope you enjoy making it. Take care and write soon,
> Love,
> Grandpa

2. On the back of this sheet, write notes to show the ten things that Jonathan needs to do to make the water garden. Make sure you write them in the correct order!

ENGLISH
STAGE 5

Instructions ◆◆
Team sports

Date set
_____

Finish by
_____

PCM
40

Name_____

You have been asked to write some instructions for playing a team sport.

1. Choose a team sport you know really well.

2. Think carefully about what is needed to play the game and how it is played.

3. Plan how to write the instructions by imagining you are describing the game to someone who has never seen it played before.

4. Write your instructions here, under the headings.

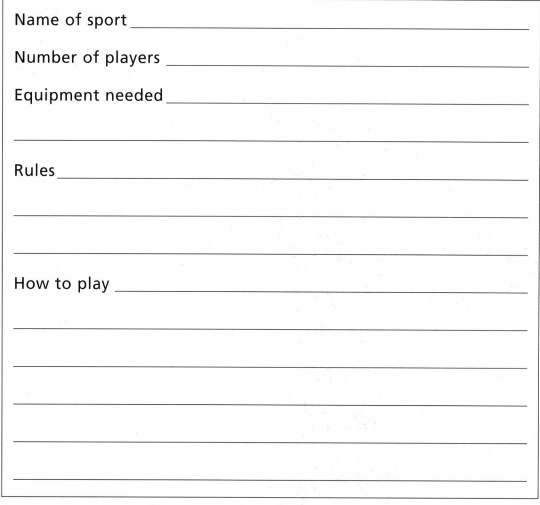

Name of sport _____

Number of players _____

Equipment needed _____

_____

Rules_____

_____

_____

How to play _____

_____

_____

_____

_____

5. Now read your instructions carefully. Are they easy to understand? Have you left anything out? Decide on any changes you need to make to improve your instructions.

Explanatory texts ◆◆
Mountain gorillas

Date set
_____

Finish by
_____

PCM
41

Name_____

1. Read the following information about Mountain Gorillas, which are an endangered species. Underline parts of the text that give us reasons why these animals are endangered.

Mountain Gorillas live in the dense forests of Central Africa. They live in groups of up to 15, headed by one large older male, and are the only apes that live on the ground. They build makeshift camps every night, either in the trees or at the base of trees.

Gorillas eat leaves, shoots, stems, roots, flowers and fruit. They need a large, undisturbed area in which to live but much of their land is being destroyed by humans who are clearing the forests for farming and building. Increasingly, people are moving into the forests to escape from areas affected by war. They cut down trees to build homes and to fuel fires for cooking, causing more forests to be destroyed.

Gorillas live for up to 30 years. Females usually have only one or sometimes two young and many of the babies born do not survive. This means gorillas have a slow rate of reproduction so the groups of gorillas do not grow in size very easily or quickly.

Sometimes, humans hunt gorillas to kill them or they capture the young ones to sell. Many African countries are now trying to prevent this happening by having armed guard patrols in the forests where the gorillas live.

2. Read through the text you have underlined again. Turn over and write in your own words four reasons why Mountain Gorillas are an endangered species.

STAGE 5

Explanatory texts ◆◆
The rainforests

Date set

Finish by

PCM
42

Name

1. Read the two texts and answer the questions on the back of this sheet.

A

The equatorial rainforests are found in the lowland areas close to the equator. Weather conditions here change very little: days and nights are very hot, there is lots of rain and the air is always moist and steamy. The people here are not as well fed, healthy or knowledgeable as we. We are more fortunate so we should try to help them as much as possible.

The rainforests contain many valuable trees but lumbering is not a major industry here. This is because it is very difficult to make roads into the forests to haul the logs out. It is not surprising, then, that most of the native people are primitive hunters and farmers.

B

Nowhere else in the world is there such a wealth of plants and animals than in the equatorial rainforests. The largest forest is in the Amazon basin but it is being eaten away by logging, land clearance for ranches and farming, mining, damming and new roads. This means that many plants and animals are now endangered.

The tribal people living here have a vast wealth of knowledge about the plants in the forests, and their medicinal properties. All these important medicines may be lost if the forests continue to be cut down. It's vital then, that the rainforests are saved from destruction.

2. One of these extracts was written in the 1950s and one is much more recent. Which do you think is the earlier extract? Why?

3. Which parts of the earlier extract could you still use to write about the rainforests today?

4. Write a list of things you should look out for when using books to find up-to-date information.

ENGLISH
STAGE 5

Name_____

Each month, the local parish produces a magazine for everyone in the village. Tom, who usually writes an article, is unwell and has asked you to write the article for him!

1. Look at Tom's notes below to write an article about the problem of irresponsible dog owners.

- Many locals upset about dog mess on footpaths.

- Some parents have complained to local council about dog mess in village playground – want a new fence built.

- Interviewed Mr Bassett – "I think we should fine owners who let their dogs make a mess. They should be made responsible!"

- Mrs Samson (shop owner) said "I think the council should put up special dog bins so dog owners can clean up any mess properly."

- Several stray dogs have been seen wandering the streets lately.

---

2. Use the back of this sheet to write the article.

- Write in sentences. Include all the facts and quotes that Tom has gathered.

- Remember to use words and phrases suitable for a parish magazine.

- Conclude your article with a general comment about what could be done to solve the problem.

Persuasive writing ◆◆

Car sales

Name_____

Nareeta's father sells cars. One day, Nareeta was asked to choose the best headline for a new car advertisement. These are the ones she had to select from:

a) The Best Purchase You Can Possibly Make This Year!

b) A Better Status Symbol Than Diamonds!

c) This Car is Simply THE BEST!

d) New Car Out Today!

e) Your Dreams Come True – No Other Car is This Good

1. Which headline do you like best? Write your reasons why.

   _____

   _____

2. Which headline do you like least? Explain why.

   _____

   _____

3. Which headline(s) are based on someone's opinion but appear to be fact?

   _____

4. Which headline do you think is the most honest? Why?

   _____

   _____

5. Choose one of the headlines and write the advertisement to go with it on the back of this sheet.

ENGLISH
STAGE 5

Persuasive writing ◆◆

Homework

Date set
_____

Finish by
_____

PCM
45

Name_____

What is your opinion on doing homework?

1. Read this extract from a poem about homework by Jack Prelutsky.

> Homework! Oh, homework!
> You're last on my list,
> I simply can't see
> why you even exist,
> if you just disappeared
> it would tickle me pink.
> Homework! Oh, homework!
> I hate you! You stink!

Do you agree with the poet? Or do you think homework is a good idea?

2. Design a leaflet that persuades others that **either** homework is important **or** it is unnecessary.

- Think up an eye-catching heading to get the reader's attention.

- Write at least four reasons for or against homework.

- Make the information sound convincing to others!

- Write the text for your leaflet below.

STAGE 5

Letters ◆◆

Home team

Date set
_____

Finish by
_____

PCM
46

Name_____

1. Read this letter that appeared in a local paper.

> Dear Editor,
>
> I am writing in response to your article about our local Under 11's Football Team. It seems that the team want to include girls! I have never heard of anything so stupid in all my life! We will not continue to win matches if the team has girls playing because they are simply not as capable as the boys – and that's a fact! Besides, what boy would want to play football with girls? It's a disgrace! Let the girls play their netball and leave the football to us men!
>
> John Hibbert

2. Now write a reply to Mr Hibbert's letter, saying whether or not you agree. State your views clearly. Continue on the back.

Write your address here:

_____

_____

_____